HOUGHTON MIFFLIN

Surprise

INVITATIONS
TO LITERACY

Houghton Mifflin Company • Boston

Atlanta • Dallas • Geneva, Illinois • Palo Alto • Princeton

Reading Is An Adventure That Makes Every Day Special

www.bookadventure.org

read.

Use the on-line "Book Finder" to find a book you want to read.

click.

After reading, return on-line to take a fun interactive quiz.

win.

For every correct answer, you can earn points. Redeem the points for prizes.

When you read, use these Reading Strategies to become a better reader.

- Predict/Infer
- Think About Words
- Self-Question

- Monitor
- Evaluate
- Summarize

HOUGHTON MIFFLIN

Surprise

Senior Authors

J. David Cooper
John J. Pikulski

Authors

Kathryn H. Au
Margarita Calderón
Jacqueline C. Comas
Marjorie Y. Lipson
J. Sabrina Mims
Susan E. Page
Sheila W. Valencia
MaryEllen Vogt

Consultants

Dolores Malcolm
Tina Saldivar
Shane Templeton

INVITATIONS TO LITERACY

Houghton Mifflin Company • Boston

Atlanta • Dallas • Geneva, Illinois • Palo Alto • Princeton

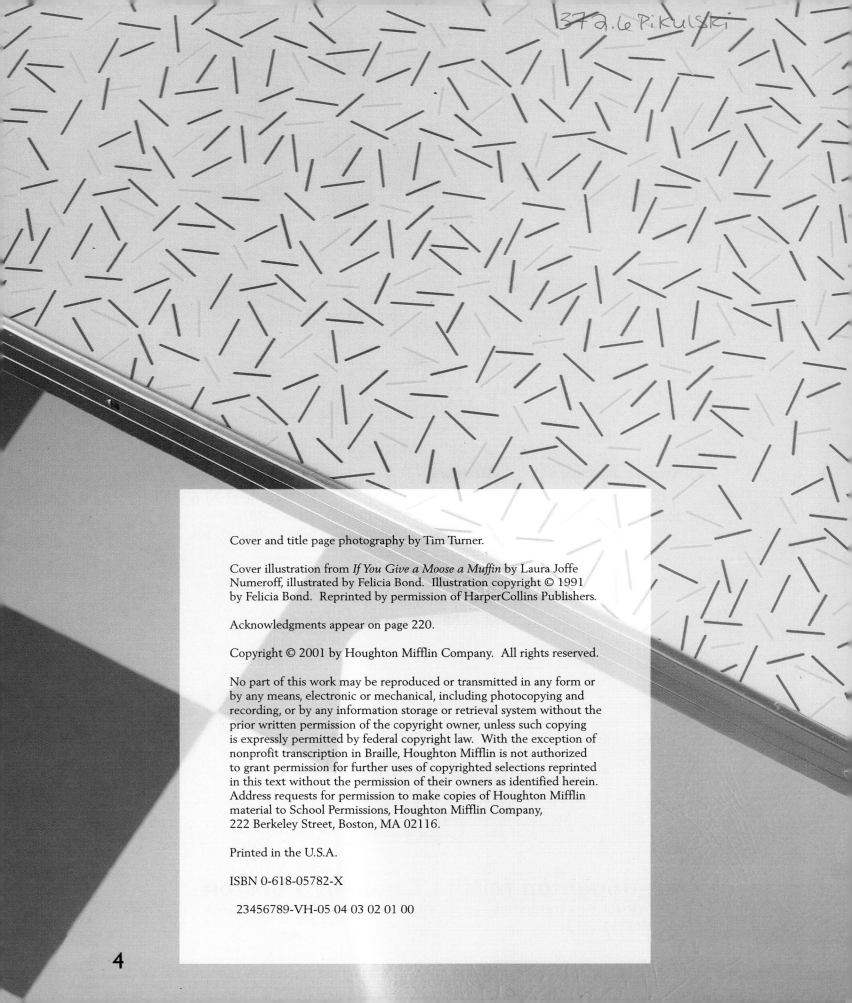

Cover and title page photography by Tim Turner.

Cover illustration from *If You Give a Moose a Muffin* by Laura Joffe
Numeroff, illustrated by Felicia Bond. Illustration copyright © 1991
by Felicia Bond. Reprinted by permission of HarperCollins Publishers.

Acknowledgments appear on page 220.

Printed in the U.S.A.

ISBN 0-618-05782-X

23456789-VH-05 04 03 02 01 00

4

Getting Started

Themes

CONTENTS

BIG BOOK PLUS

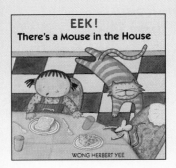

EEK! There's a Mouse in the House
a story written and illustrated by
Wong Herbert Yee
In the same book . . .
a song in Spanish and English, animal
riddles, and a guessing game

Anthology

PAPERBACK **PLUS**

Big and Little

BIG BOOK PLUS

If the Dinosaurs Came Back
a story written and illustrated by
Bernard Most

In the same book . . .
a science activity, more facts about
dinosaurs, and a dinosaur poem

Anthology

PAPERBACK **PLUS**

Meet Eileen Roe

Eileen Roe loves to spend special times with her family. One thing her family loves is going boating together. This picture shows Ms. Roe and her two children, Samantha and Jason, on a boat dock.

Meet Robert Casilla

When Robert Casilla needs help with his drawings, he usually asks his family. His son, Robert, Jr., was the model for the little boy in *Con Mi Hermano/With My Brother*. Like the little boy in the book, Robert, Jr., speaks English and Spanish.

Con Mi Hermano

With My Brother

by/por Eileen Roe • illustrations by/ilustraciones por Robert Casilla

My brother is bigger and older than I.
He goes to school on the bus,

Mi hermano es más grande y mayor que yo.
Él va a la escuela en el ómnibus escolar

and delivers newspapers in the afternoon,

y reparte los periódicos por la tarde

and plays ball at the park on Saturdays.

y juega a la pelota en el parque los sábados.

He doesn't always have time to play with me.

A veces no tiene tiempo de jugar conmigo.

But sometimes, I sit outside on the
steps and wait for him to come home.
When he sees me, he smiles and
calls my name.

Pero a veces me siento en la escalera
y espero a que llegue a casa.
Cuando me ve, sonríe y me saluda.

20

I run to him.
He grabs me
and we wrestle on the grass.
I always win.

Corro hacia él.
Él me agarra
y luchamos en el pasto.
Yo siempre gano.

We walk down to the playground together,
my brother and I.

Caminamos juntos al patio de recreo,
mi hermano y yo.

We play catch,

Jugamos a la pelota

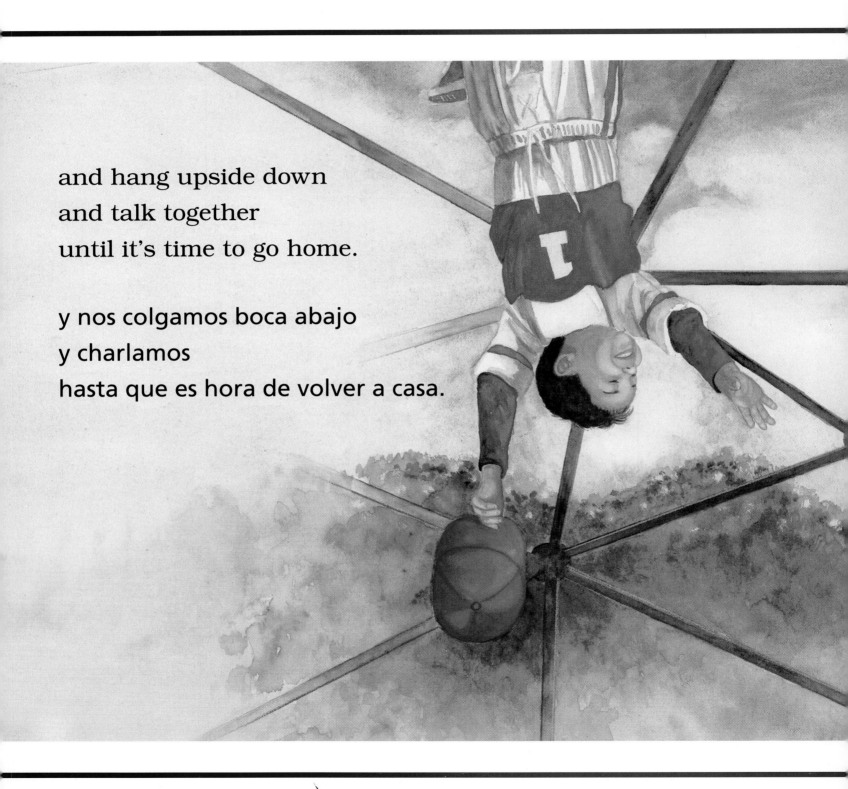

and hang upside down
and talk together
until it's time to go home.

y nos colgamos boca abajo
y charlamos
hasta que es hora de volver a casa.

And sometimes in the evening,
when he finishes his homework,
we will do a puzzle together

Y a veces por la tarde,
cuando él termina sus tareas,
trabajamos juntos en un rompecabezas

or I'll climb up on his lap
and we will read our favorite books

o me subo a sus rodillas
para leer nuestros libros favoritos

and sometimes he will say I'm getting too heavy,
that soon I'll be too big
to sit on his lap.

y a veces me dice que ya peso tanto
que pronto estaré demasiado grande
para sentarme en sus rodillas.

But that's okay
because maybe then
I'll be big enough
to go to school on the bus,

Pero eso está bien
porque quizás para entonces
estaré bastante grande
para ir a la escuela en el ómnibus escolar

and deliver newspapers in the afternoon,

y repartir los periódicos por la tarde

and play ball at the park on Saturdays

y jugar a la pelota en el parque los sábados

with my brother.

con mi hermano.

What's Your Game?

Make a game you'd like to play with someone special. Then show a friend how to play.

41

Unexpected Guests

EEK!
There's a Mouse in the House

BIG BOOK PLUS

WONG HERBERT YEE

**EEK! There's a Mouse
in the House**

by Wong Herbert Yee

44

Table of Contents

More Books You Can Read!

PHONICS BOOKSHELF
Nate and His Cape

PHONICS BOOKSHELF
Mike's Grapevines

PHONICS BOOKSHELF
Big Mule's Rules

Nancy Shaw
Sheep in a Shop
Illustrated by Margot Apple

WATCH ME READ
A Great Place for Llama

WATCH ME READ
Never Wake a Sleeping Snake

WATCH ME READ
A Tune for My Mother

PAPERBACK **PLUS**

Mercer Mayer

has written and illustrated over two hundred books for children. He says, "I tell stories with pictures, and quite often I even add words."

46

written and illustrated by MERCER MAYER

There used to be an alligator under my bed.

When it was time to go to sleep,
I had to be very careful

because I knew he was there.

But whenever I looked,
he hid . . . or something.

So I'd call Mom and Dad.

But they never saw it.

It was up to me.
I just had to do something
about that alligator.

57

So I went to the kitchen
to get some alligator bait.

I filled a paper bag full
of things alligators like to eat.

I put a peanut butter sandwich,
some fruit, and the last piece
of pie in the garage.

I put cookies down the hall.

I left fresh vegetables on the stairs.

I put a soda and some candy
next to my bed.
Then I watched and waited.

64

Sure enough, out he came
to get something to eat.

Then I hid in the hall closet.

I followed him down the stairs.

I followed him down the hall.

When he crawled into the garage,

I slammed the door and locked it.

Then I went to bed.

There wasn't even any mess to clean up.

Now that there is an alligator in the garage,
I wonder if my dad will have any trouble
getting in his car tomorrow morning.

I'll just leave him a note.

Make a Sign

What kind of sign would you make to warn someone about the alligator? Make a sign with a friend.

NO people!
Alligator inside

DANGER!
There's an alligator here.

March 29, 1994

Dear Ranger Rick,

One afternoon we had a really wild yard! First a pair of ducks came up our driveway. Right after that, we saw a black snake slithering across our backyard.

Later on, a pigeon with a band around its leg came flying into the yard. And it landed on my dad's head!

Sincerely,
Elise Moon
Tucson, Arizona

Ranger Rick
August 1994
National Wildlife Federation

WILD VISITORS

One afternoon we had a really *wild* yard! First a pair of ducks came up our driveway. Right after that, we saw a black snake slithering across our backyard.

Later on, a pigeon with a band around its leg came flying into the yard. And it landed on my dad's head!

Elise Moon; Tucson, AZ

RUNNING INTO A ROADRUNNER

I liked the story on roadrunners in your August issue last year. Today

78

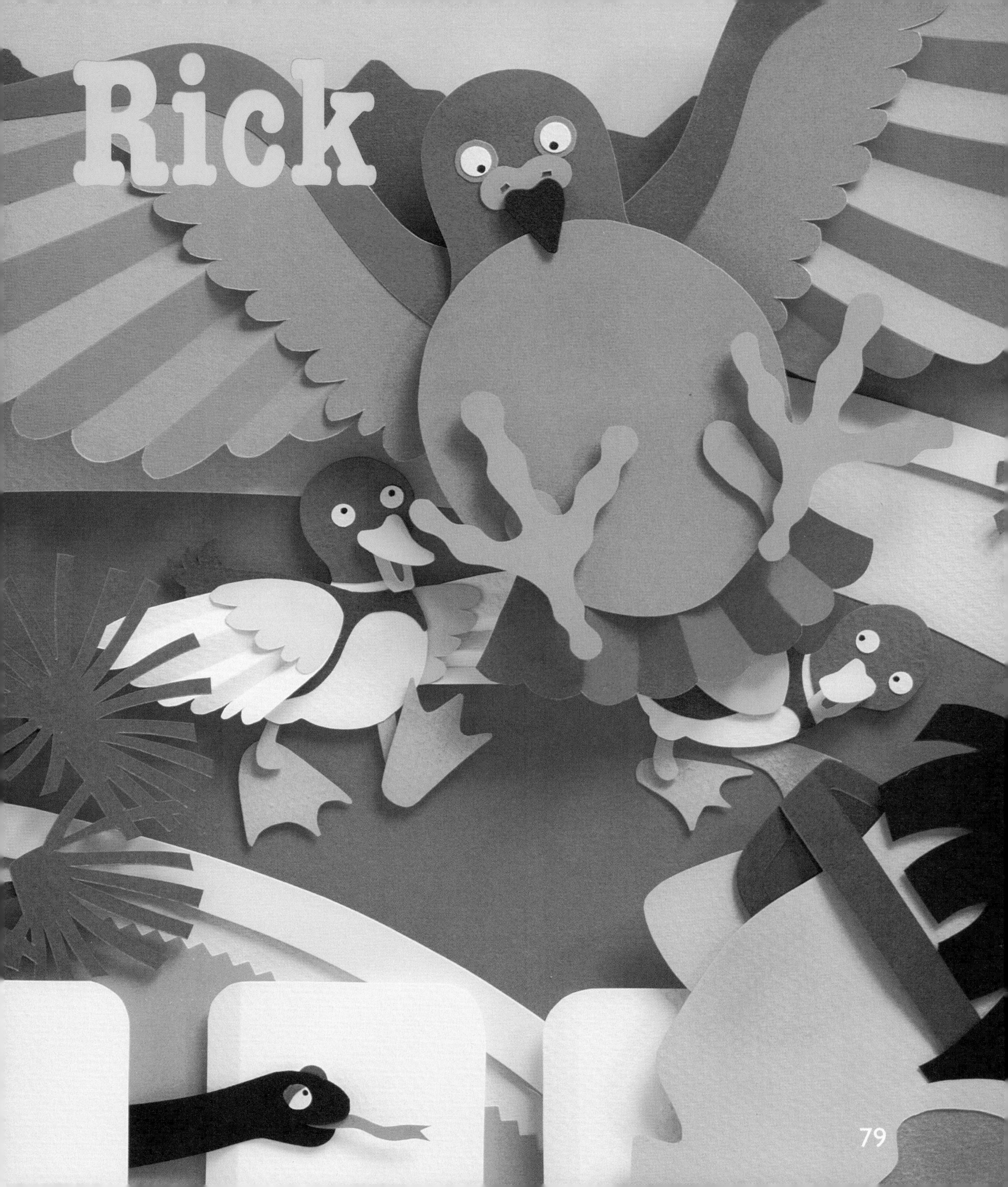
Rick

Dear Robert Anthony

A Letter by Joshua Henry Mishaan

You just read a letter about wild animals in Elise Moon's backyard. Now read about what happens inside Joshua's house!

Joshua Henry Mishaan

Lorenzo Loya Elementary School
El Paso, Texas

Joshua wrote this letter to his cousin Robert Anthony. Joshua loves animals. He wants to be a farmer or veterinarian when he grows up.

August 23, 1994

Dear Robert Anthony,

   I am writing this letter to tell you about something I saw. I saw JoJo, my hamster, doing something strange.

   JoJo got out of his cage. I had to search for him all over the house. Guess where I found him? He was in the closet eating my daddy's black rubber sandals. I wish you could have seen him too.

                    Your cousin,
                    Joshua

Count the

This Navajo rug by Linda Nez contains over fifty animals.

Animals

mountain lion

How many of each animal can you find in the rug?

bear

bird

Laura Joffe Numeroff

If You Give a Mouse a Cookie

Felicia Bond

Laura Joffe Numeroff also wrote *If You Give a Mouse a Cookie*. When she is not writing, she is usually at the library or bookstore, collecting books.

Felicia Bond did the drawings for *If You Give a Mouse a Cookie*. She listens to music when she draws. And sometimes her cats visit her at work!

If you give a moose a muffin,

he'll want some jam to go with it.

So you'll bring out some of your
mother's homemade blackberry jam.

When he's finished eating
the muffin, he'll want another.

And another.

90

And another.
When they're all gone,
he'll ask you to make more.

91

You'll have to go to the store
to get some muffin mix.

He'll want to go with you.

When he opens the door and feels how chilly it is, he'll ask to borrow a sweater.

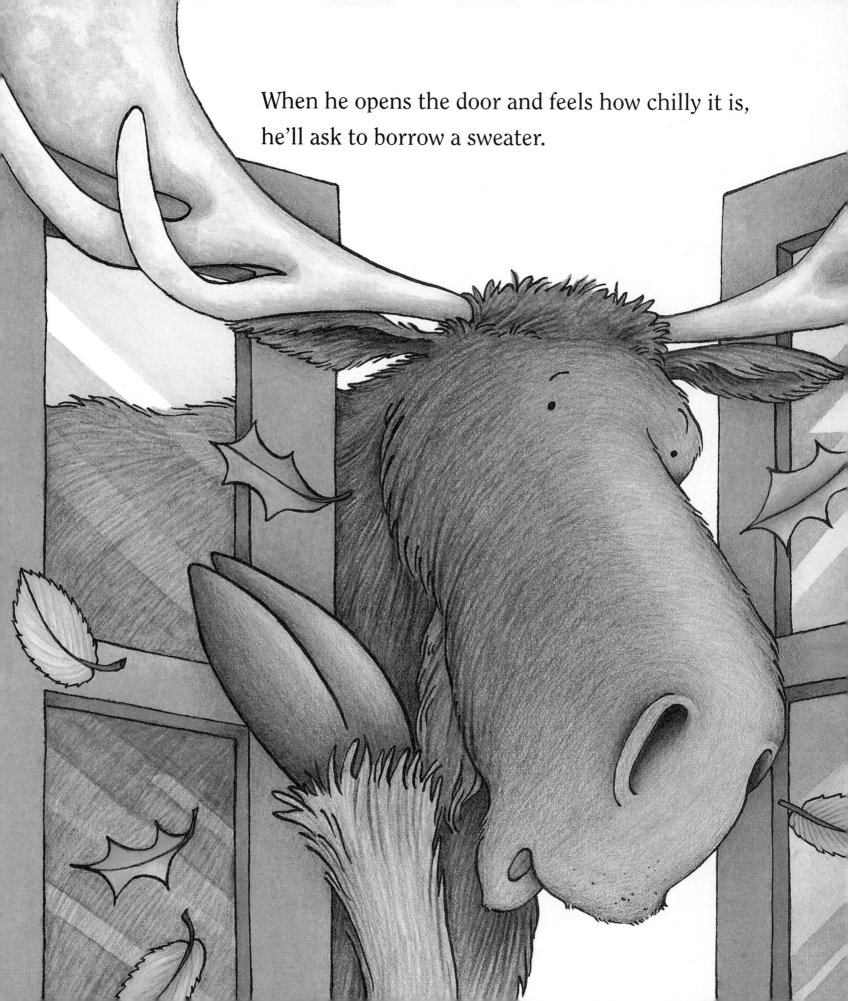

When he puts the sweater on, he'll notice one of the buttons is loose.

He'll ask for a needle and thread.

94

He'll start sewing.
The button will remind him of the
puppets his grandmother
used to make.

So he'll ask for some old socks.

He'll make sock puppets.

When they're done, he'll want to
put on a puppet show.

He'll need some cardboard
and paints.

Then he'll ask you to help make the scenery.

When the scenery is finished, he'll get
behind the couch.
But his antlers will stick out.

So he'll ask for something to cover them up.

You'll bring him a sheet from your bed.

When he sees the sheet, he'll remember
he wants to be a ghost for Halloween.

He'll try it on and shout,

"BOO!"

It'll scare him
so much, he'll knock
over the paints.

105

So he'll use the sheet
to clean up the mess.

Then he'll ask for some soap to wash it out.

He'll probably want to hang the sheet up to dry.

He'll go outside to put it
on the clothesline.

108

When he's out in the yard, he'll see
your mother's blackberry bushes.

Seeing the blackberries
will remind him of
her jam.

110

He'll probably ask you for some.

111

And chances are . . .

if you give him the jam,

he'll want a muffin to go with it.

Act It Out!

Act out your favorite parts of the story with a partner. Decide who will be the boy and who will be the moose. Then have the class guess what you are doing.

MOOSE

mother moose
with twins

116

Moose live in forests. They eat leaves, twigs, and bark. In the summer, moose wade into lakes or ponds. They munch on water plants.

father moose

Moose calves are born in spring. Often, twins are born. The mother moose takes care of her calves for about a year. Then the young moose are on their own.

These two moose are both males. You can tell because they have antlers.

The moose's antlers begin to grow in spring. They grow all summer. In the winter, the antlers fall off. Moose grow new antlers every year.

WILD FACTS

These chimpanzees are playing ring-around-the-rosy.

Wild lambs
sometimes
bump heads
for fun. Ouch!

Are the kangaroos
dancing? No, they are
pretending to fight.

Elephant

The elephant carries a great big trunk.
He never packs it with clothes.
It has no lock and it has no key,
But he takes it wherever he goes.

Anonymous

Always Be Kind to Animals

Always be kind to animals,
Morning, noon, and night;
For animals have feelings too,
And furthermore, they bite.

by John Gardner

Big and Little

If the dinosaurs came back
by Bernard Most

126

Table of Contents

More Books You Can Read!

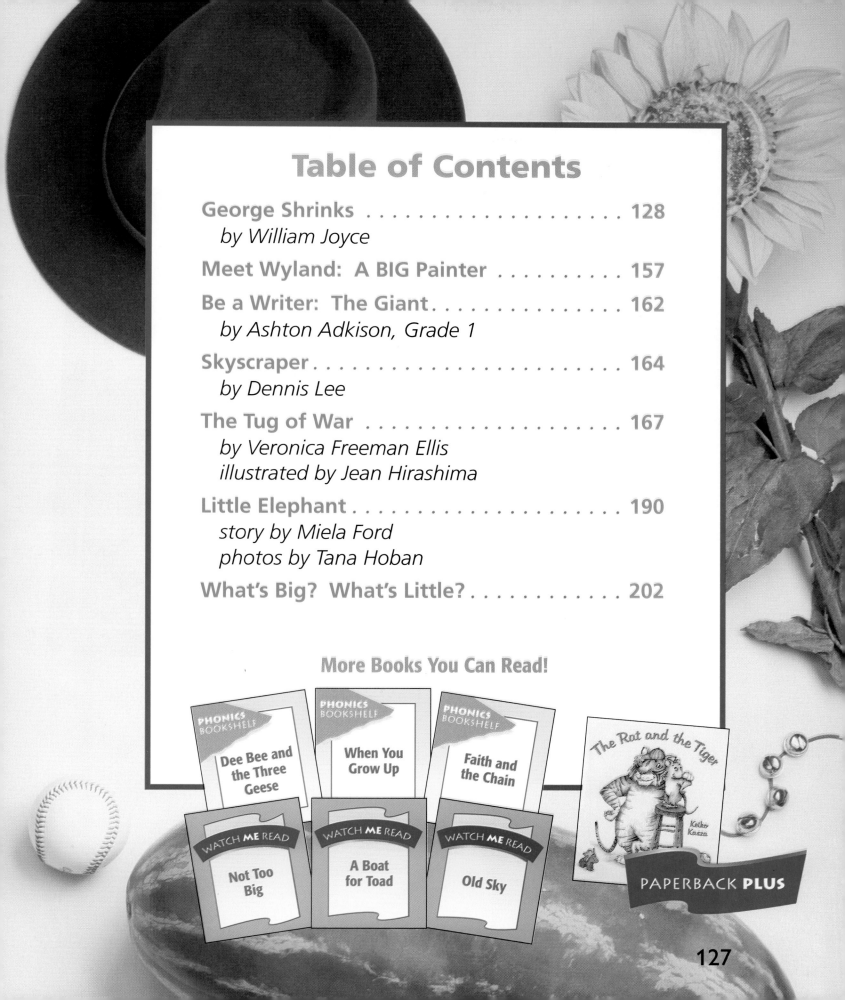

PHONICS BOOKSHELF
Dee Bee and the Three Geese

PHONICS BOOKSHELF
When You Grow Up

PHONICS BOOKSHELF
Faith and the Chain

WATCH **ME** READ
Not Too Big

WATCH **ME** READ
A Boat for Toad

WATCH **ME** READ
Old Sky

The Rat and the Tiger
Keiko Kasza

PAPERBACK **PLUS**

One day, while his mother and father were out,
George dreamt he was small,
and when he woke up he found out it was true.

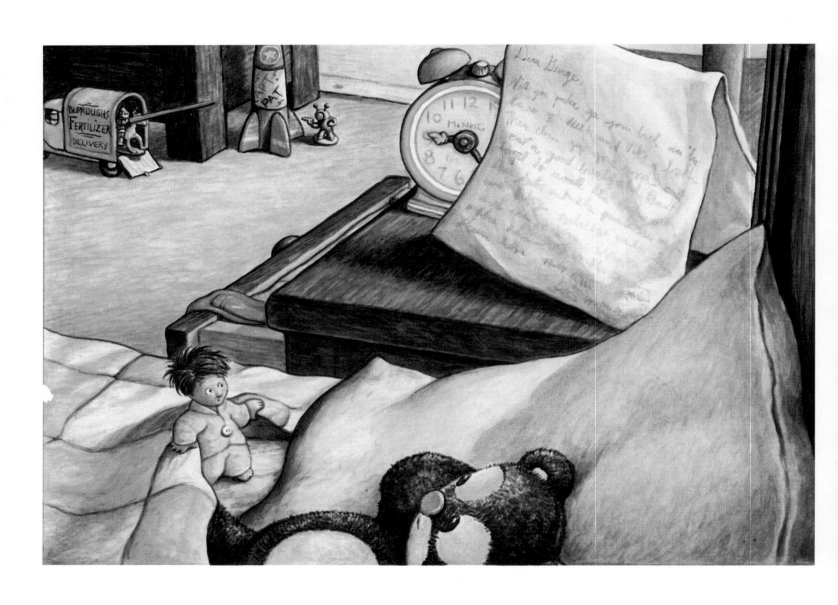

His parents had left him a note:

"Dear George," it said. "When you wake up,

please make your bed,

brush your teeth,

and take a bath.

Then clean up your room

and go get your little brother.

Eat a good breakfast,

and don't forget to wash the dishes, dear.

Take out the garbage,

and play quietly.

Make sure you water the plants

and feed the fish.

Then check the mail

and get some fresh air.

146

Try to stay out of trouble,

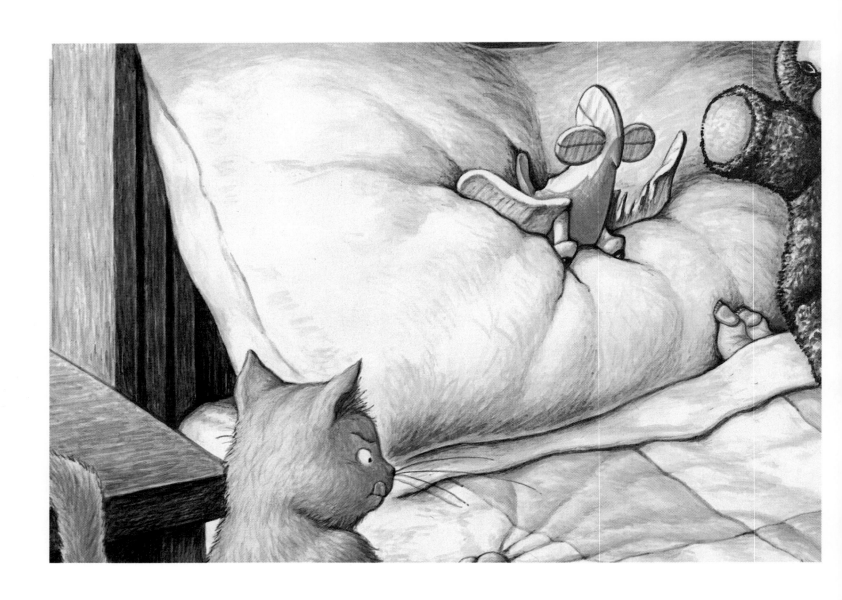

and we'll be home soon.

Love, Mom and Dad."

Meet William Joyce

George Shrinks was William Joyce's first picture book. Mr. Joyce says that when he draws people for his books, his family helps him with his drawings. They pose for him as he draws.

William Joyce as a boy

George Grows

What would George's day have been like if he had woken up BIG instead of little? Write a story about George's BIG adventures.

Meet Wyland: A BIG Painter

Wow! Wyland is an artist who paints **BIG** whales on the sides of TALL buildings. This type of painting is called a **mural**.

Why do you paint whales?

I paint whales because I want people to learn more about them.

What do you do to get ready?

Before I paint, I try to go out and see the whales. I study them and where they swim.

How do you begin painting?

I cover the entire wall with ocean. After that, I still don't know what I'm going to paint. But then I look into that ocean and think where the whales would swim.

What do you do next?

I do a light painting of the whale. This is called ghosting. Then I'll fill in different areas of the whale.

159

How do you finish your painting?

From there, I add more details until the painting is done.

Snorkelift

Can you describe one of your paintings?

This painting is in Alaska. The wall was very smooth. I used five colors: blue, green, white, black, and yellow. On the left, there are ribbon seals. In the middle, the three big black whales with white on their chins are bowhead whales. There are also four white beluga whales. And on the right, you see some spotted seals on a little ice floe.

The Giant

A Description by Ashton Adkison

Ashton wrote about something really BIG!
See how she describes her BIG friend.

Ashton Adkison

Northwest Rankin
   Elementary School
Brandon, Mississippi

Ashton enjoys school a lot! She reads stories to her little brother and writes letters to pen pals. Ashton wrote about her giant when she was in the first grade. The giant has blonde hair — just like Ashton!

162

The Giant

She is very big. Her head is huge.
And her feet are humungous. Her
clothes are very big. Her fingers are
very, very big. Her bow is huge.

SKYSCRAPER

Skyscraper, skyscraper,

Scrape me some sky:

Tickle the sun

While the stars go by.

Tickle the stars

While the sun's climbing high,

Then skyscraper, skyscraper

Scrape me some sky.

by Dennis Lee

Space Needle
Seattle

164

Transamerica Pyramid
San Francisco

Chrysler Building
New York

Sears Tower
Chicago

Meet Veronica Freeman Ellis

When Veronica Freeman Ellis was a little girl in Liberia, she grew up listening to and telling stories. Today, she writes stories because she can share many wonderful events with children.

Meet Jean Hirashima

You might have seen Jean Hirashima's art before. She used to make drawings for greeting cards. Ms. Hirashima now lives in New York City.

About This Story

In Liberia, the storyteller starts by saying, "Once upon a time." The audience shows that it's ready to listen by repeating the last word, "Time!" Then the story begins!

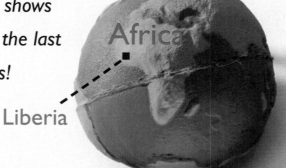

Africa

Liberia

166

The Tug of War

a play adapted by

Veronica Freeman Ellis

illustrated by Jean Hirashima

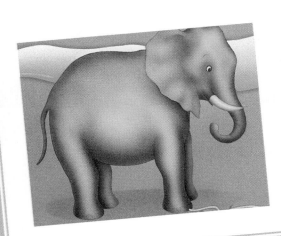

Storyteller: Once upon a time . . .

Audience: Time!

Storyteller: A little possum named Tapidou had a big problem. The mighty Elephant and Hippo always teased him because he was so little.

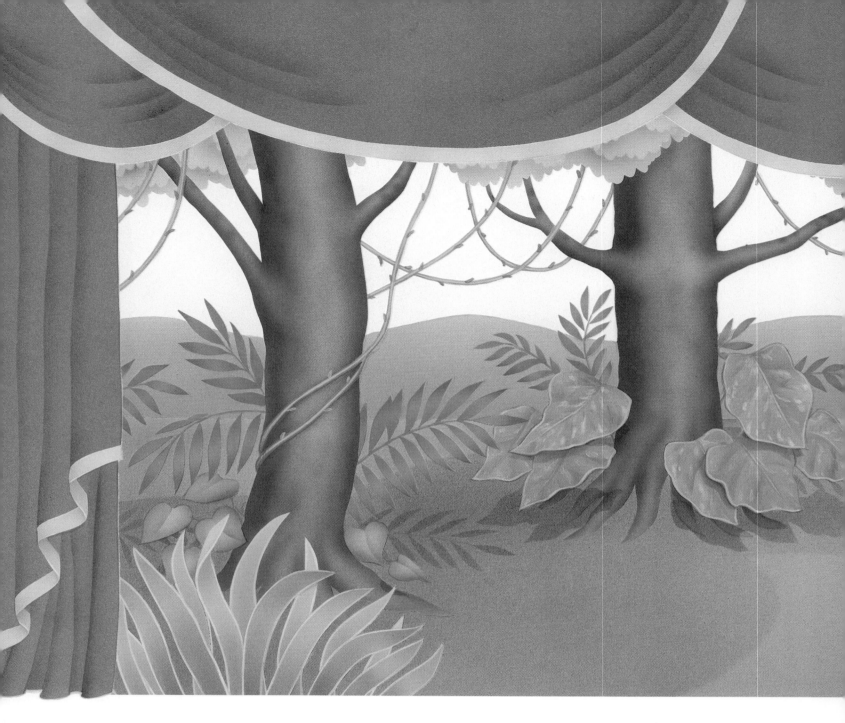

Storyteller: One morning Tapidou was walking in the rain forest. Along came the mighty Elephant and nearly stepped on him.

Tapidou:
(shouting)

Hey, big friend! Watch where you go!
You mustn't step on those below.

170

Elephant:
(laughing)   Look — it's little Tapidou!
Why, you're no bigger than a stone!

Tapidou: Next to you, I may be small.
But I'm the strongest one of all!

Elephant: Don't make me laugh. You're much too
tiny to be that strong.

171

Scene 2
The river

Storyteller: The next day Tapidou was walking by the river. Along came the mighty Hippo and nearly bumped him into the water.

Tapidou:
(shouting)   Hey, big friend! Watch where you go! You mustn't step on those below.

Hippo: It's little Tapidou! Why, you're no bigger than my ear!

Tapidou: Next to you, I may be small.
But I'm the strongest one of all!

Hippo: You? You must be joking. You're much too tiny to be that strong.

Storyteller: Months went by, and Elephant and Hippo still teased Tapidou whenever they saw him.

Hippo and Elephant: Ha! There's that little Tapidou. He still thinks he's as strong as we are!

Storyteller: Tapidou was growing tired of all this teasing.
One day, he thought of a plan.

Tapidou: I won't let them make fun of me.
(to audience)   I'll play a trick on them — you'll see!

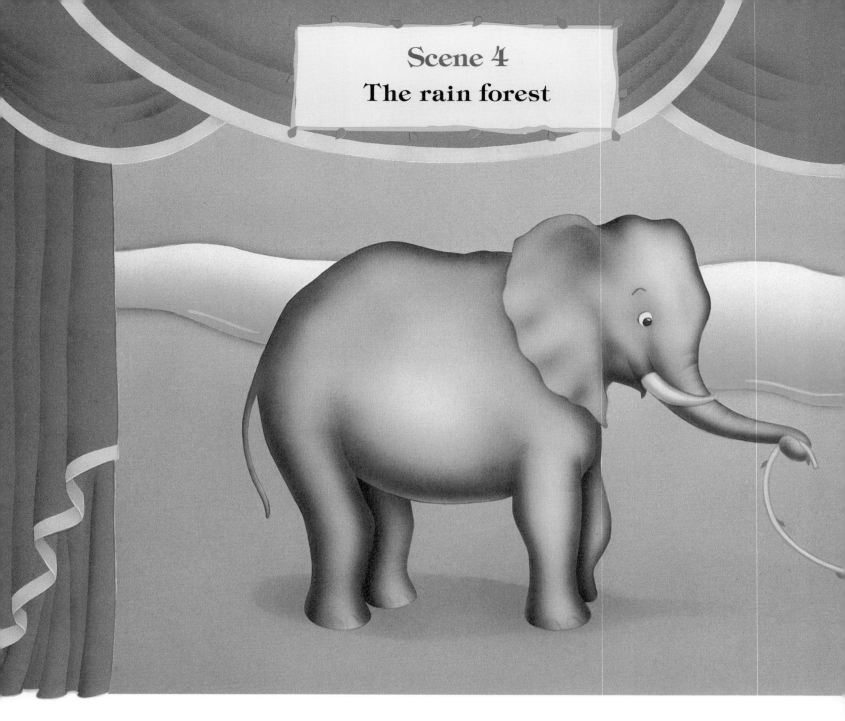

Scene 4
The rain forest

Tapidou:	It's time to put you to the test.
	I'll PROVE I'm stronger than the rest!
Elephant:	How will you prove that, Tapidou?
Tapidou:	A tug of war, my elephant friend,
	will bring your teasing to an end!

176

Tapidou:	Let me show you. See this vine?
	Here is your end. Here is mine.
	Who can tug on this vine longer?
	If it's you, then YOU are stronger.
Elephant:	I'm ready. This contest will be an easy one!

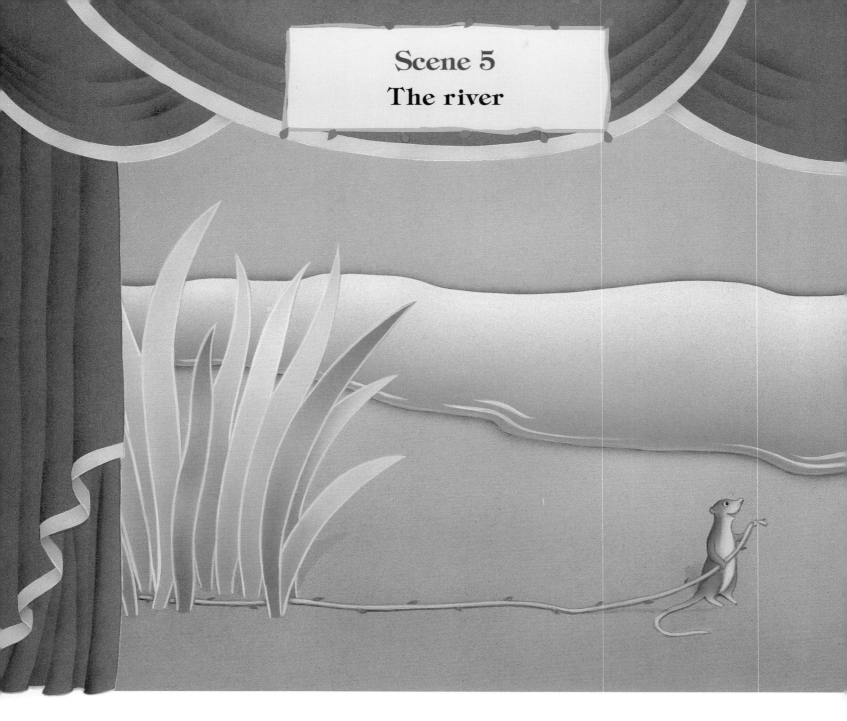

Scene 5
The river

Tapidou:	It's time to put you to the test.
	I'll PROVE I'm stronger than the rest!
Hippo:	How will you prove that, Tapidou?
Tapidou:	A tug of war, my hippo friend,
	will bring your teasing to an end!

178

Tapidou: Let me show you. See this vine?
Here is your end. Here is mine.
Who can tug on this vine longer?
If it's you, then YOU are stronger.

Hippo: Let's do it. You're an easy match for me!

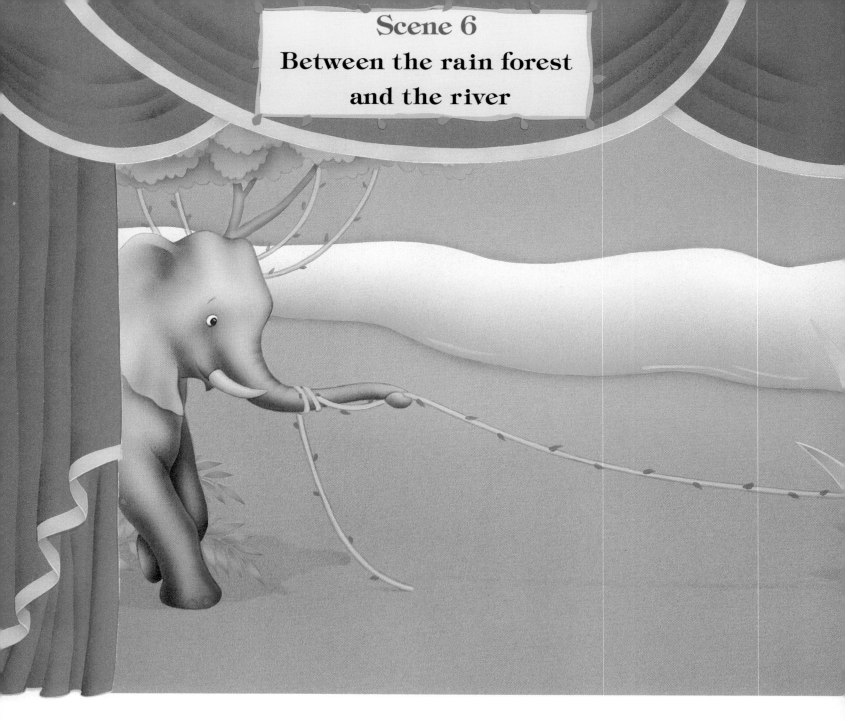

Storyteller: Elephant took his end of the vine and went to the forest. Hippo took his end of the vine and went to the river.

180

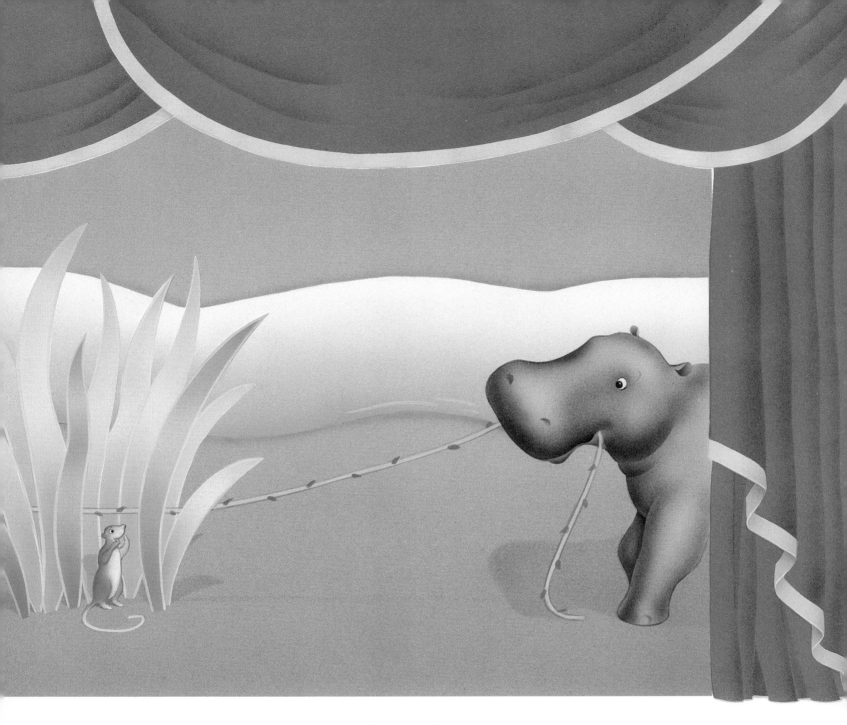

Tapidou:
(shouting and hiding)

One, two, three, four!

It's time to start the TUG OF WAR!

Storyteller: Elephant pulled with all his might.

Elephant: That little Tapidou is stronger than I thought!
(groaning)

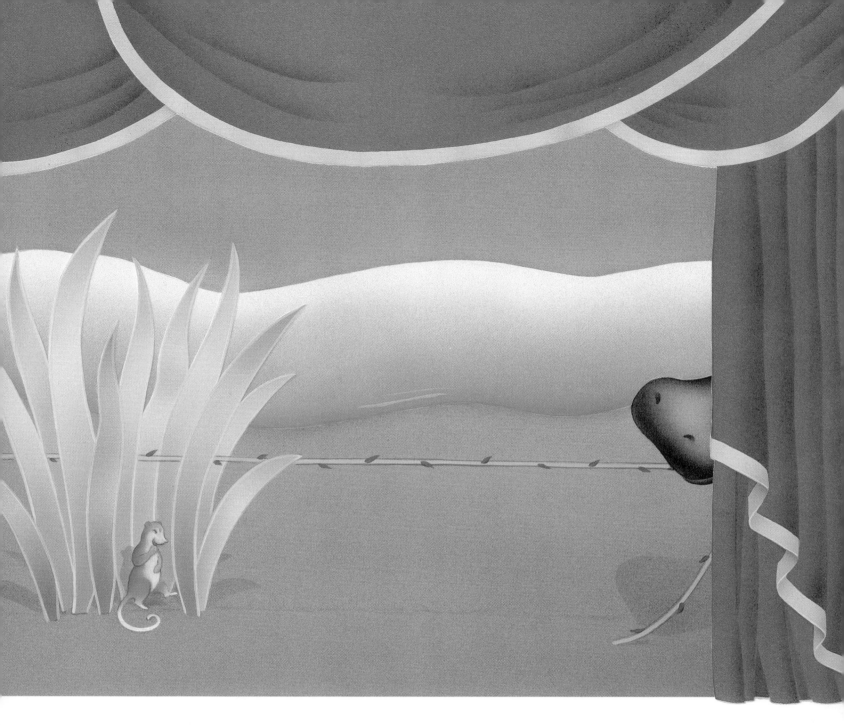

Storyteller:	And Hippo pulled, too.
Hippo: *(groaning)*	How could such a tiny possum be so strong?
Storyteller:	Elephant and Hippo pulled on the vine all day long.

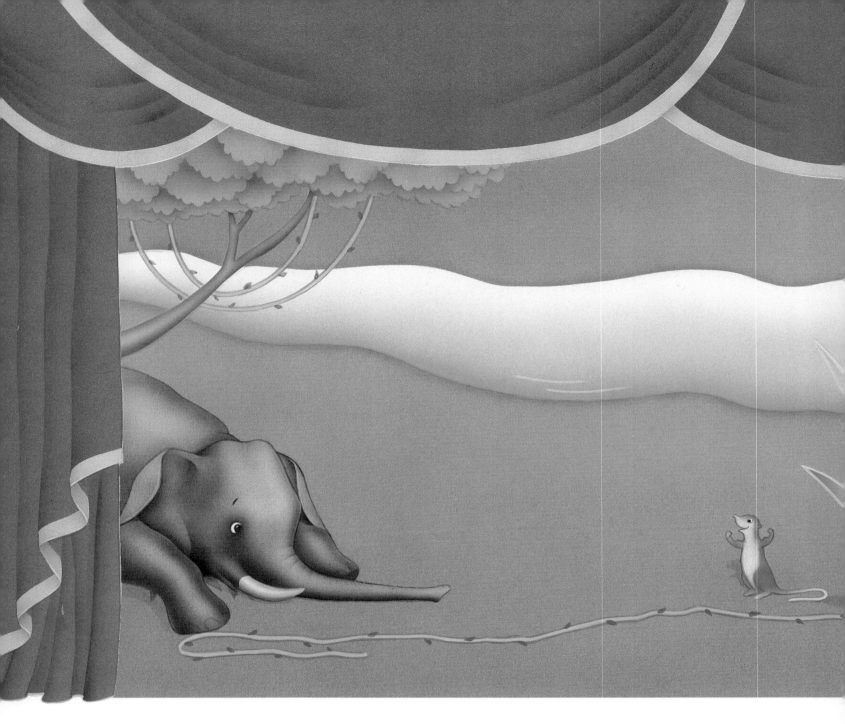

Storyteller: At last Elephant and Hippo grew tired. . . .

They both dropped the vine at the same time
and fell to the ground.

Storyteller: Elephant went to find Tapidou.

Elephant: I tugged as long as I could. Tapidou, you were right. You're the strongest one of all!

186

Storyteller: Hippo went to find Tapidou.

Hippo: I tugged as long as I could. Tapidou, you were right. You're the strongest one of all!

Scene 7
The rain forest

Storyteller:	From then on, Hippo and Elephant never teased Tapidou again.
Hippo:	Good night, friend!
Elephant:	Good night, friend!
Tapidou:	Good night, all!
Storyteller:	And that's THE END!

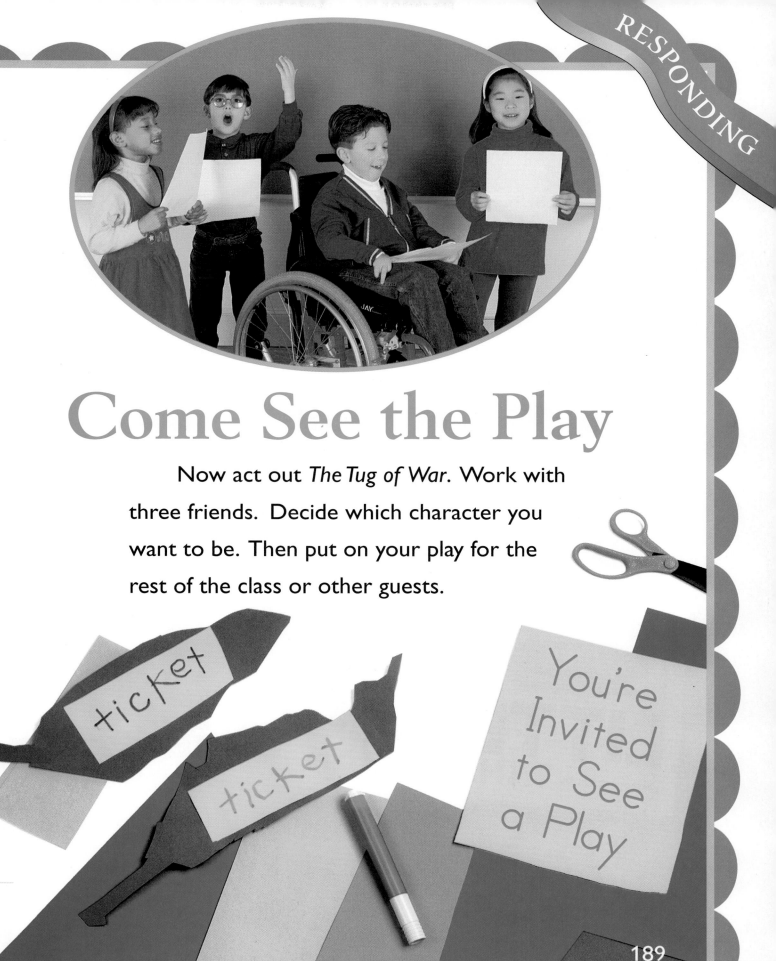

Come See the Play

Now act out *The Tug of War*. Work with three friends. Decide which character you want to be. Then put on your play for the rest of the class or other guests.

ticket

ticket

You're Invited to See a Play

LITTLE ELEPHANT

photographs by **TANA HOBAN** story by **MIELA FORD**

I am a little elephant.

This is my mother.

She lets me play in the water.

First one toe,

then two.

193

A big splash.

Lots of bubbles.

Up goes my trunk.

Swing it around.

Under I go.

Can you see me?

Here I am.

Time to get out.

This is hard.

Oops!

Can I make it?

Yes, I can!

Hurry now.

Where is my mother?

Waiting for me!

What's **Big?**

little **tree**

big tree

What's Little?

big clock

little clock

little steps

big steps

204

Look at the people playing music.

Name the **big** things you see.

Name the **little** things you see.

A

air   **Air** is all around you. You can't see **air**, but you can feel it when the wind blows.

alligator   An **alligator** is a kind of animal: The **alligator** has a long tail that helps it swim.

antler   An **antler** is one of the horns of a deer or moose: The deer's **antlers** are on top of its head.

audience   The **audience** watched the play. The **audience** clapped because they liked the play.

B

bait   **Bait** is what you use to catch something, like an animal: Roberto used worms as **bait** to catch fish.

blackberry   A **blackberry** is a small fruit that grows on a bush: We picked **blackberries** to bring to our picnic.

breakfast   The food you eat in the morning is called **breakfast**: My family likes to eat cereal for **breakfast**.

C

careful   When you are **careful**, you think about what you are doing and use care: Be **careful** and look both ways before crossing the street.

clothesline   After they wash their clothes, some people hang them up to dry on a **clothesline**: We put our wet clothes on the **clothesline** outside our window.

contest   A **contest** is a kind of game to see who can win: The girls had a **contest** to see who could jump higher.

D

dream   People sometimes **dream** while they are sleeping at night: Last night, I **dreamt** that I was as small as a mouse.

garage A **garage** is a place to keep a car: Mom puts the car into the **garage** when she comes home from work.

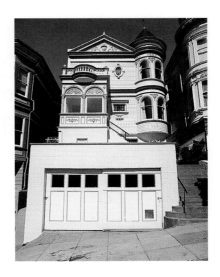

jam **Jam** is a sweet food made from fruit: You can put **jam** on bread or muffins.

joke When you **joke**, you say something to make someone laugh: Matt likes to **joke** with his friends. He was **joking** when he said his dog was from outer space.

laugh
My friends **laugh** when I tell a funny story. They keep on **laughing** when I make funny faces.

M

mighty
Someone who is big and strong is **mighty**: Both the elephant and the lion are **mighty** animals.

moose
A **moose** is the largest kind of deer: The **moose** was eating leaves in the forest.

muffin   A **muffin** is a type of bread.
It is about as big as a cupcake:
I like to eat a **muffin** with
butter and jam for breakfast.

P

parent   A mother is a **parent**. A father is a **parent**,
too: George calls his **parents** Mom and Dad.

peanut butter   **Peanut butter** is a food
that is made from peanuts.
You can eat it with bread:
Nina likes **peanut butter**
and jelly sandwiches.

possum   A **possum** is a small animal with fur. Another name for **possum** is **opossum**: We saw a **possum** climb a tree.

probably   It will **probably** rain today, so I will bring an umbrella.

problem   You have a **problem** when things do not happen in the way they should: Lee had a **problem** when she missed the school bus. Her father helped her take care of the **problem** by driving her to school in the car.

prove   When you **prove** something you show it is true: I can **prove** that I can run faster than you by winning a race.

pull

To **pull** is to bring something closer to you: She **pulled** the wagon to move it closer to her.

puppet

A **puppet** is a toy that can look like an animal or a person: We made all kinds of **puppets** to retell our story.

Q

quietly

To do something **quietly** means to do it without making much sound: Kim played **quietly** because he didn't want to wake up his family.

rain forest   A **rain forest** is a place with many trees, plants, and animals. It rains a lot in a **rain forest**.

remind   Some people need someone to **remind** them about important things so that they won't forget: No one has to **remind** me that my birthday is in the summer.

scenery   We drew and painted **scenery** for our class play. The **scenery** shows trees and clouds, so people will know that the story takes place outside.

sew   When you **sew**, you put pieces of cloth together using a needle and some thread: Mikka is **sewing** clothes to wear for the dance.

slam   To **slam** a door is to shut it hard with a noise: My father didn't like it when I **slammed** the door. It made too much noise!

soda   A **soda** is a sweet, cold drink: I drink milk with my meals, but I can have a **soda** after school.

sweater   A **sweater** is clothing that helps keep you warm: I wear my **sweater** on cold days.

tease   Most people think you should not **tease**, or make fun of, others: The boy **teased** his friend because he was too little to ride a bike.

trouble   When something is hard to do, it may cause **trouble:** My legs are so long that I have **trouble** fitting them under my desk.

true   It is **true** that rain is water that falls from the sky. It is not **true** that pigs can talk.

tug of war   A **tug of war** is a pulling game: In the **tug of war**, the first graders pulled against the second graders. The first graders won!

vine   A **vine** is a plant that is long and thin. A **vine** looks like a long rope: The monkey can use the **vine** to swing from tree to tree.

W

wonder   When you **wonder** whether something will happen or not, you are not sure: My friends and I **wonder** if it will snow tonight.

GLOSARIO

E

escuela

(school)

La **escuela** es el lugar donde los estudiantes aprenden cosas: En la **escuela** aprendí cómo leer un cuento.

P

patio de recreo

(playground)

Un **patio de recreo** es un lugar donde puedes jugar: Cada día, los niños juegan al fútbol en el **patio de recreo.**

218

periódico

(newspaper)

Las noticias se escriben en el **periódico**: Mi mamá lee dos **periódicos** cada día. Ella quiere saber todo lo que pasa en la ciudad.

R

rompecabezas

(puzzle)

Para hacer un **rompecabezas**, hay que encajar todas las piezas: Raúl ha perdido unas piezas de su **rompecabezas**. Ahora no puede completarlo.

T

tareas

(homework)

Hacer las **tareas** es hacer trabajo de la escuela en casa: Tengo que hacer mis **tareas** de matemáticas antes de salir a jugar.

ACKNOWLEDGMENTS

For each of the selections listed below, grateful acknowledgment is made for permission to excerpt and/or reprint original or copyrighted material, as follows:

Selections

Con Mi Hermano/With My Brother, by Eileen Roe, illustrated by Robert Casilla. Text copyright © 1991 by Eileen Roe. Illustrations copyright © 1991 by Robert Casilla. Reprinted by permission of Macmillan Books for Young Readers, Simon & Schuster Children's Publishing Division.

George Shrinks, by William Joyce. Copyright © 1985 by William Joyce. Reprinted by permission of HarperCollins Publishers.

If You Give a Moose a Muffin, by Laura Joffe Numeroff, illustrated by Felicia Bond. Text copyright © 1991 by Laura Numeroff. Illustrations copyright © 1991 by Felicia Bond. Reprinted by permission of HarperCollins Publishers.

Little Elephant, by Meila Ford, photos by Tana Hoban. Text copyright © 1994 by Meila Ford. Photographs copyright © 1994 by Tana Hoban. Reprinted by permission of Greenwillow Books, a division of William Morrow & Company, Inc.

"Moose," from July, Series II issue of *Your Big Backyard* magazine. Copyright © 1981 by The National Wildlife Federation. Reprinted by permission.

There's an Alligator Under My Bed, written and illustrated by Mercer Mayer. Copyright © 1987 by Mercer Mayer. Reprinted by permission of Dial Books for Young Readers, a division of Penguin USA.

"Wild Visitors," from August 1994 *Ranger Rick* magazine. Copyright © 1994 by The National Wildlife Federation. Reprinted by permission.

Poetry

"Always Be Kind to Animals," from *A Child's Bestiary*, by John Gardner. Copyright © 1975 by Boskydell Artists. Reprinted by permission of Georges Borchardt, Inc. for the estate of John Gardner.

"Elephant," traditional.

"Skyscraper," from *Alligator Pie,* by Dennis Lee. Copyright © 1974 by Dennis Lee. Reprinted by permission of the author.

Special thanks to Wyland and Kathleen Rogers of the Venema Group, Los Angeles, California.

Special thanks to the following teachers whose students' compositions appear in the Be a Writer features in this level: Isabelle Mishaan, Lorenzo Loya Elementary School, El Paso, Texas; Diane Jacobsen, Northwest Rankin Elementary School, Brandon, Mississippi.

CREDITS

Illustration   5, 11–40 Robert Casilla; 6, 44 Wong Herbert Yee; 7, 45 Margot Apple; 1, 2 (bottom), 6, 47–76 Mercer Mayer; 78–79 Judith Moffat; 81 Joshua Henry Mishaan; 7, 85–114 Felicia Bond; 8, 126 Bernard Most; 9, 127 Keiko Kasza; 2 (left center), 8, 128–154 William Joyce; 163 Ashton Adkison; 165 Jim Gordon; 9, 167–188 Jean Hirashima

Assignment Photography   41, 189 Banta Digital Group; 46 (inset), 166 (bottom) Kindra Clineff; 10–11, 42–47, 84–85, 115 (border), 116–119, 124–128, 155, 166–167, 190–191 Tony Scarpetta; 41, 77 (inset), 115 (inset), 156, 189, 202 (top left), 203 (bottom right), 204 (top right), 205 Tracey Wheeler

Photography   2 Ana Venegas/© National Geographic Society (t); © Wyland Studios Inc. (mr) 7 Thase Daniel (cover) 10 Courtesy of Eileen Roe (t); Courtesy of Robert Casilla 42 © 1994 Zefa Germany/The Stock Market (inset, l) 44 © Ben Osborne/© Tony Stone Images/Chicago Inc. (br) 78 Frans Lanting/Minden Pictures (cover) 80 Courtesy of Joshua Henry Mishaan 82 Jerry Jacka Photography 83 © Daniel J. Cox/Liaison International (bl); © Stephen Krasemann/Tony Stone Images/Chicago Inc. (br) 84 Courtesy of HarperCollins, Laura Geringer Books (t); courtesy of Felicia Bond (b) 116–117 © Stephen Krasemann/DRK Photo 116 Thase Daniel (cover) 117 William C. Fraser 118–119 Helen Rhode/Big Backyard 120 © Art Wolfe/Art Wolfe (l); Jane Goodall Institute (r) 121 Tom Walker (l); Toni Angermayer/Photo Researchers (r) 122 Alan M. Detrick/Photo Researchers (t); Ana M. Venegas/© National Geographic Society (l) 123 Ana M. Venegas/© National Geographic Society (tl); Craig Hammell/The Stock Market (tr); Lucy Perron/Photo Researchers (br) 155 Courtesy of William Joyce 157 Daniel R. Westergren/© National Geographic Society 158–161 © Wyland Studios Inc. 162 Courtesy of Ashton Adkison 164–165 Larry Dale Gordon/The Image Bank 166 Courtesy of Veronica Freeman Ellis (t); Courtesy of Jean Hirashima (b) 202 Ken Briggs/Tony Stone Images/Chicago Inc. (r) 203 © David Brownell/The Image Bank (m) 204 © Will & Deni McIntyre/Photo Researchers (b) 206 Don Landwerhl/The Image Bank (b) 208 Joanna McCarthy/The Image Bank (t) 209 Donald Dietz/Stock Boston (t) 210 Andy Caulfield/The Image Bank (t); Charles Campbell/Westlight (b) 212 Lynn Stone/The Image Bank (t) 213 Craig Hammel/The Stock Market (t) 214 J. Carmichael Jr./The Image Bank (t); Lawrence Migdale/Stock Boston (b) 216 Robert Dammrich/Tony Stone Images (b) 217 J. Carmichael Jr./The Image Bank (t) 218 Donald Dietz/Stock Boston (t); Paulo Fridman/Liaison International (b)

Here's what visitors to our Web site said about stories in *Surprise.*

I like *Con Mi Hermano/With My Brother.* The best part is when his brother comes home and plays with the younger brother. I like it when they play with puzzles and read books together. One day I'll be big enough to play in the park and ride the bus by myself.

Mark Anthony Fernandez, Hawaii

If You Give a Moose a Muffin made me feel happy because they picked up their mess. It made me laugh when the illustrator drew the moose with a little purse. I liked it when they painted the scenery because it was funny.

Levi Watson, Maine

Post your reviews in the

Kids' Clubhouse

at

www.eduplace.com